CALIFORNIA
Here We Come!

BY
PAM MUÑOZ RYAN

ILLUSTRATED BY
KAY SALEM

Charlesbridge

To my wonderful dad, Don Bell, who refinishes California

Thank you to Michele Horner and Pat Ward for their assistance with the research for this book

—P. M. R.

To Michelle Atiles, a gifted teacher whose spirit, dedication, and patience made this book possible

Thank you to Juliana McIntyre, who designed, redesigned, edited, art directed, and baby-sat me through this book

—K. S.

Published by Charlesbridge Publishing
85 Main Street, Watertown, MA 02472 • (617) 926-0329
www.charlesbridge.com

Printed in the United States of America
(hc) 10 9 8 7 6 5 4 3 2
(sc) 10 9 8 7 6 5 4 3 2 1

Library of Congress Cataloging-in-Publication Data
Ryan, Pam Muñoz.
California here we come!/by Pam Muñoz Ryan; illustrated by Kay Salem.
p.   cm.
Summary: Takes the reader on an imaginary trip through California while offering information about the history and geography of this varied region with its numerous historic sites.
ISBN 0-88106-881-0 (reinforced for library use)
ISBN 0-88106-880-2 (softcover)
1. California—History—Juvenile literature. 2. Historic sites—California—Juvenile literature.
3. California Trail—Juvenile literature. 4. California—Description and travel—Juvenile literature. [1. California—Description and travel. 2. California—History. 3. Historic sites—California.] I. Salem, Kay, ill. II. Title.
F861.3.R93   1997
979.4—dc20   95-9471

The paintings in this book are done in Spectralite acrylic airbrush color and Windsor & Newton watercolor on Strathmore illustration board.
The display type and text type were set in Cyclone and Poppl Laudatio.
Color separations were made by Bright Arts Graphics, Singapore.
Printed and bound by Worzalla Publishing Company, Stevens Point, Wisconsin
This book was printed on recycled paper.
Production supervision by Brian G. Walker
Designed by Diane M. Earley

Hello, I am Carmen.
Get ready to take
A guided tour
Of this treasure-filled state!

There are valleys and deserts
And mountains and coast.
Which region do you think
That you will like most?

scenic route

INTERSTATE CALIFORNIA 5

Golden California VISITOR'S GUIDE

We'll start in the south
Of this golden land,
In fair San Diego,
Where vistas are grand.

In this coastal city
There's plenty to do.
There are beaches and surfing
And a world-famous zoo.

hummingbird

dolphin

poinsettia

* Thousands of years ago, Asian hunters migrated to North America through what is now Alaska. Their descendants, the first Californians, later became known as Native Americans. * In the 1500s, Juan Rodríquez Cabrillo landed in San Diego and claimed the area for Spain. Later, San Diego became the site of the first West Coast settlement, on Presidio Hill. Today, this area has been restored in Old Town State Park. * Eucalyptus trees from Australia were planted in San Diego in the 1860s for their hard wood and oil. They are now a distinctive feature of San Diego's landscape. * Many ships have stopped in San Diego's harbor over the past 400 years. Today, it is home to a U.S. Navy port. * The vintage wooden Giant Dipper Roller Coaster in Mission Beach is a National Historic Landmark. * Poinsettia plants are grown at the Paul Ecke Poinsettia Ranch in Encinitas, north of San Diego. From there, they are shipped to all parts of the nation. *

San Diego

Juan Rodríquez Cabrillo

GIANT DIPPER SAN DIEGO

eucalyptus tree

navy ship

San Juan Capistrano
Is where we will learn
About a quaint village
Where swallows return.

Junípero Serra
Stopped here on his way
To build a grand mission
From adobe clay.

cliff swallow nest

cliff swallow

San Juan Capistrano

Father Junípero Serra

bougainvillea

* Spain sent missionaries to California in 1769 to establish churches and to colonize the Native Americans who lived on the frontier. Junípero Serra, a Spanish priest, is called "the Father of California." He founded nine of the twenty-one missions that reach from San Diego to Sonoma, including San Juan Capistrano. Each mission was built "one day's journey by foot" from the next, along El Camino Real, or "the Royal Road." This road is still marked by the missions' staff-and-bell symbol. * The Shoshoni Indians who lived here were renamed "Juaneño" by the missionaries. Their mission products included cured hides, dipped candles, and soap. * The swallows of Capistrano leave each year around October 23rd and return the next spring, around the 19th of March. * San Juan Capistrano, in Orange County, was once surrounded by citrus groves. Today, most of the area is housing developments. * The state flower, the golden poppy, is symbolic of the state mineral, gold, and the fair weather in California. *

El Camino Real staff and bell

cured hides

soap

dipped candles

orange tree

Next is Los Angeles
And famed Hollywood.
You can visit the places
Where movie stars stood!

This "City of Angels"
Has lots to explore:
Museums and tar pits
And amusements galore!

HOLLYWOOD

Los Angeles

California condor

Griffith Observatory

* In 1542, Cabrillo continued on his voyage and sighted San Pedro, the present harbor of Los Angeles. He saw smoke from the campfires of many Native American villages and called the harbor Bahía de los Fumos (Bay of Smokes). * In 1781, forty-four Mexican settlers established Pueblo de Nuestra Señora la Reina de Los Angeles de Porciúncula, which means "Town of Our Lady the Queen of the Angels of Porciúncula." Now it is simply called Los Angeles. * The La Brea pits are bogs of oil and tar that trapped prehistoric animals in this area. Thousands of fossils have been recovered from the tar pits, including the saber-toothed tiger, the state fossil. * Since 1890, the Tournament of Roses Parade has been an annual New Year's Day event in Pasadena. It includes elaborate floats decorated with flowers. * Griffith Park, home of Griffith Observatory, is the largest urban park in California. * The endangered California condor lives along the central coastal mountains, from Monterey County to north Los Angeles County. *

movies and television

Tournament OF Roses

imperial mammoth

saber-toothed tiger

Now, the Channel Islands!
We'll take a boat out,
And cruise these blue waters
To glimpse a whale's spout.

Here in the Pacific
Among the kelp strips
Are playful sea otters
And the ghosts of old ships.

humpback whale

Channel Islands

sea lion

double-crested cormorant

scuba diver

* The Channel Islands stretch off the coast of California from Santa Barbara to the San Clemente area. Writer Scott O'Dell wrote about the island of San Nicolas in his famous novel, *Island of the Blue Dolphins*. * Pirates used to visit the Channel Islands. Several shipwrecks lie at the bottom of the sea—some people think there is still sunken treasure there. Many scuba divers still search for it near these islands. * The waters around these islands were once full of sea otters. Fur trappers hunted them until they were almost extinct. Today, biologists have brought otters back to the islands. Hopefully, sea otters will make their home here again. * The Chumash Indians of this area were known and respected for their canoe-building skills. Their *tomols* were made with wooden planks that were tied together and caulked with tar. These canoes, which were painted red, were strong enough to withstand the Pacific Ocean waters. *

sea otter

Chumash tomol

Spanish galleon

As we travel north
We approach Monterey
And the bold, craggy rocks
That surround the bay.

When sardines were plenty
Some years ago,
The day's catch was sold
Here on Cannery Row.

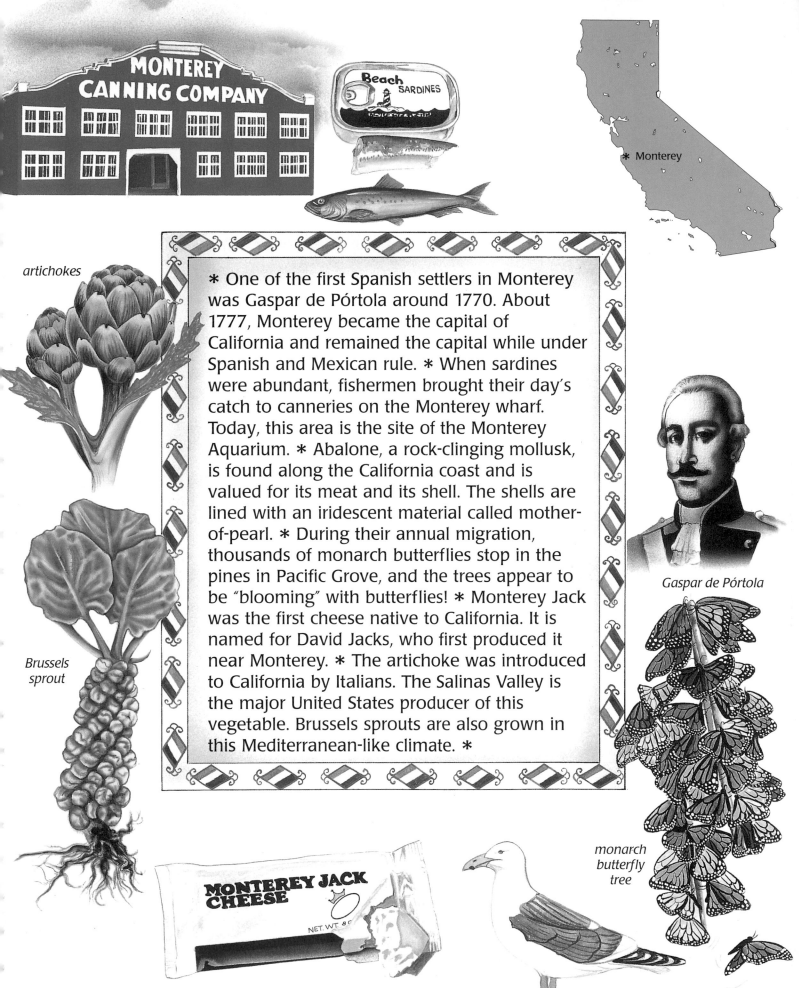

artichokes

Brussels sprout

MONTEREY CANNING COMPANY

Beach SARDINES

* Monterey

* One of the first Spanish settlers in Monterey was Gaspar de Pórtola around 1770. About 1777, Monterey became the capital of California and remained the capital while under Spanish and Mexican rule. * When sardines were abundant, fishermen brought their day's catch to canneries on the Monterey wharf. Today, this area is the site of the Monterey Aquarium. * Abalone, a rock-clinging mollusk, is found along the California coast and is valued for its meat and its shell. The shells are lined with an iridescent material called mother-of-pearl. * During their annual migration, thousands of monarch butterflies stop in the pines in Pacific Grove, and the trees appear to be "blooming" with butterflies! * Monterey Jack was the first cheese native to California. It is named for David Jacks, who first produced it near Monterey. * The artichoke was introduced to California by Italians. The Salinas Valley is the major United States producer of this vegetable. Brussels sprouts are also grown in this Mediterranean-like climate. *

Gaspar de Pórtola

MONTEREY JACK CHEESE
NET. WT. 8 oz

monarch butterfly tree

western gull

Let's stop in "The City,"
San Francisco's the name.
Here, morning fog lingers
And winds bring the rain.

Cable cars hurry
Up one hill and down
And tourists eat lunch
In old Chinatown.

Golden
Gate
Bridge

Mark
Twain

San Francisco *

great egret

* Until it was renamed in 1847, San Francisco was called Yerba Buena, which means "good herb," after the wild mint that grew there. * The San Francisco cable cars are State Historical Landmarks. They are the only ones left in the world! * "Mark twain," which means "two fathoms deep," was a term that Samuel Clemens used while working on Mississippi riverboats. Clemens, who used Mark Twain as his pen name, wrote many stories about California and the West. * In 1906, an earthquake and fire destroyed much of San Francisco, but its citizens eventually rebuilt the city. The phoenix, a mythical bird reborn from its own ashes, is San Francisco's symbol. * Domingo Ghirardelli began making chocolate in San Francisco in 1852, and you can still watch it being made in Ghirardelli Square. One of Ghirardelli's chocolate bars weighs five pounds! * San Francisco's Golden Gate Bridge is almost seven miles long. Maintenance crews continually refurbish the bridge using 10,000 gallons of orange paint every year. *

*Ghirardelli
chocolate*

phoenix

gateway to Chinatown

Once in Sonoma,
Under rebels' command,
Settlers claimed a republic
For Destiny's Land.

They made a new flag
To be flown everywhere
With one stripe and one star
And a fierce grizzly bear.

* Sonoma

* The land we call California has been claimed by many people: the Native Americans, the Spanish, the Mexicans, and the American settlers. * "Manifest destiny" was a journalistic phrase first used in the 1840s. It meant that the United States should claim the land from the Atlantic Ocean to the Pacific Ocean. This idea fueled arguments between the United States and Mexico about who owned California. * In 1846, American settlers peacefully took over the Mexican fort in Sonoma from General Mariano Vallejo. They carried a homemade flag featuring a grizzly bear as a symbol of strength and proclaimed California a new republic. This was called the Bear Flag Revolt. * Since the mid-1800s, Sonoma Valley and Napa Valley have been leaders in California wine making, or viticulture. * The golden eagle and the bald eagle are native to California. Once there were so many eagles in California that over twenty places were named after them. * The Coast Miwok, the original inhabitants of the Sonoma area, made willow frame houses, thatched with tule. *

Miwok brush shelter

golden eagle

General Mariano Vallejo

Bear Flag monument

grizzly bear

Napa Valley

This state has a motto
From prospectors' lore.
Miners yelled it when spotting
That rich golden ore.

"Eureka!" they cheered.
What a jubilant sound!
It's also the name
Of this northwestern town.

brown pelican

Dungeness crab

* Eureka

sequoia

redwood

* Eureka means "I have found it!" * Eureka was founded in 1850 as a gold-mining town. It later became a logging and fishing center. In Humboldt Bay you can catch rockfish, Dungeness crab, salmon, shrimp, and oysters. * In the 1800s, William Carson, a lumber baron, built a large home with a distinctive architecture. Today, many houses in the Eureka area are built or preserved in the same Victorian style as the William Carson mansion. * Redwood National Park is home to the California redwoods. Some are over 1,000 years old and can weigh 500 tons. Although these are the tallest trees in the world, one of their pinecones, which may contain up to sixty seeds, would fit in a tablespoon. * Many Native American tribes revered the grizzly bear. One tribe of this area, the Hupa, believed that the spirits of grandmothers lived inside the grizzlies. For this reason, they never killed them. Due to hunting and trapping by other groups, the grizzly bear is now considered extinct in California. *

pinecone

William Carson house

Hupa purse

logging

We're in Sacramento
At the capitol dome.
This delta city
Is the governor's home.

The Pony Express
Once delivered the post
From St. Joseph, Missouri,
To this distant West Coast.

Pony Express

Sacramento
*

Central
Pacific Railroad

Theodore Judah

* Sacramento is the capital of California. The capitol building is surrounded by 800 trees and shrubs from around the world. Camellia plants, with their delicate blooms, also flourish in Sacramento, which claims to be the camellia capital of the world. * Sacramento is located where the American and Sacramento Rivers come together. The Sacramento delta is a triangular plain that has been created from deposits of earth and sand from the rivers. This delta is full of waterways, tule swamps, marshes, and wet peat: a perfect place to grow produce! * In the early 1860s, before telephones, telegraphs, or railroads, people in California communicated with those in the rest of the country by Pony Express. Horseback riders relayed messages from the East to Sacramento, the West Coast terminus. * In the late 1800s, Theodore Judah hoped to connect the country by transcontinental railroad. He promoted the Central Pacific Railroad Company, which began laying track in Sacramento toward the East. *

camellia

tomatoes

mourning dove

asparagus

sugar beets

Here in Coloma
The story is told
Of James W. Marshall,
Who discovered pure gold.

Then the forty-niners rushed
To mine every hill
And pan every stream
That was near Sutter's Mill.

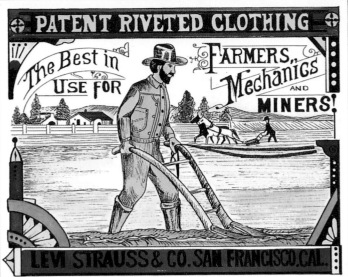

PATENT RIVETED CLOTHING

The Best in USE FOR

FARMERS, Mechanics AND MINERS!

LEVI STRAUSS & CO. SAN FRANCISCO, CAL.

Coloma *

California holly

harmonica

banjo

belted kingfisher

* James W. Marshall and John Sutter went into business together in 1847 to build a sawmill. John Sutter provided land and money, and James Marshall agreed to build the mill. In 1848, before the sawmill was finished, James Marshall discovered gold at the mill site. By 1849, thousands of prospectors had rushed to California to strike it rich. Mining towns cropped up all over the lower mountain elevations, including Oroville, Rough and Ready, Gold Run, El Dorado, and Fiddletown.
* Many people made money by selling goods during the gold rush. At a factory in San Francisco, Levi Strauss made heavy-duty pants out of denim. He reinforced the seams with copper rivets and sold them to miners and farmers. Today, they are still known as Levi's® jeans. * The banjo and the harmonica were familiar musical instruments during the gold rush days. They were easy to cart along, and they brought music and merriment to the sometimes lonesome and difficult lives of the prospectors. *

James Marshall

John Sutter

Now east to Yosemite
Where sequoias abound
And magnificent monoliths
Rise from the ground!

Once, ice-age glaciers
Carved their way through
And created a valley
With a breathtaking view!

YOSEMITE
NATIONAL PARK

lupine

John Muir

Yosemite Valley

mule deer

* Yosemite Valley, located in the Sierra Nevada mountains, is known for its rock cliffs and waterfalls. There are more waterfalls in Yosemite than anywhere else in the world! * A monolith is a single block of stone that is unusually large. Yosemite has monoliths that are the size of mountains. Some of Yosemite's majestic rock forms include Half Dome, Three Brothers, El Capitan, and Cathedral Rocks. * John Muir, a naturalist who loved the beauty of the outdoors, was dedicated to protecting Yosemite's natural resources. * Have you ever heard of Hetch Hetchy Valley? It was another beautiful valley in Yosemite, but it could not be protected from development. A dam was built, and the valley is now under water. It has become a reservoir to supply water to San Francisco. * Yosemite is home to the American black bear, the Steller's jay, and abundant mule deer. * The Mono Lake Paiutes, a tribe in the Yosemite area, are known for their beautiful, intricate baskets. *

giant sequoias

Steller's jay

black bear

Hetch Hetchy Valley

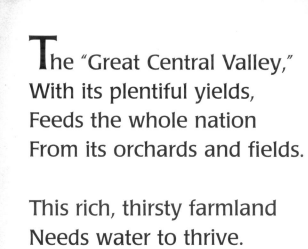

The "Great Central Valley,"
With its plentiful yields,
Feeds the whole nation
From its orchards and fields.

This rich, thirsty farmland
Needs water to thrive.
Canals, pumps, and dams
Keep this valley alive.

farmworker

Central Valley

aqueduct

California black oak

cotton

* The "Great Central Valley," named Valle Grande by the Spanish, is California's prime region for agriculture and livestock. Although it has been called the most fertile farmland in the world, there is little natural water here. The California aqueduct, a series of reservoirs, pumps, and cement channels, carries water over 400 miles from the Sacramento delta to this and other parched areas. * After working as a laborer in the Central Valley, Cesar Chavez started the National Farm Workers Union. He organized and demonstrated to improve the working conditions of farmworkers. * Once, approximately fifty tribes of Yokut Indians occupied the Central Valley. One staple of their diet, the acorn, was gathered from oak trees, stored, husked, and then used to make flour for a kind of pudding. * Oil is one of California's most important industries and resources, especially in the San Joaquin Valley. If you look across the valley, you will see many oil derricks and oil pumps. *

Yokut
bearing basket

oil "horse" pump

cantaloupe

California valley quail

plums

carrots

onions

almonds

Here's Death Valley's desert
Of salt pan and sand,
Where dust devils twirl
Across wild, crusty land.

We're in Furnace Creek,
A sweltering spot.
It's over one-twenty!
Are you getting hot?

twenty-mule-team wagon train

Death
Valley

Joshua
tree

* Death Valley is the hottest and driest place in North America. It only gets about 1½ inches of rain per year. * Here, you can stand in Badwater, the lowest point in the Western Hemisphere at 282 feet below sea level. In the distance, you can see Mount Whitney, the highest point in the continental United States at 14,494 feet above sea level. * Borax, a mineral that is mined in Death Valley, is a salt used to make many products, including laundry detergent. Years ago, borax was mined and then hauled by twenty-mule teams to the Mojave railroad station. * Prickly pear cactuses are common in California. They come in many varieties, including Beavertail, Bunny Ears, and Teddy Bear. Some have edible "pears." * Joshua trees are giant yucca plants that can grow up to fifty feet tall. They have thick, twisted branches with few leaves and giant, waxlike flowers. Joshua Tree National Monument, east of Palm Springs, is a protected area that features these unusual trees. *

Mount Whitney

kangaroo rat

panamint daisy

wild burro

sage
grouse

Finally, Palm Springs
And the end of our ride.
Let's put up our feet
And enjoy the poolside.

Now we can relax
From our travel routine
And remember the
Treasure-filled places we've seen.

date palm

NATIONAL DATE FESTIVAL

Palm Springs *

* Palm Springs, located in California's Colorado Desert, is a favorite resort town for golfers and people who like warm winters. * Have you ever felt an earthquake? Earthquakes sometimes occur along the San Andreas Fault. This fault zone runs from Mexico, through California near Palm Springs, and north past Punta Gorda in northern California. Some earthquakes are strong, but most are small and barely noticeable. * Like streamlined windmills, more than 4,000 wind turbines generate electricity near Palm Springs. * The town of Indio hosts the annual National Date Festival, which features the exotic fruit of the date palm tree. This event also features camel and ostrich races. * The Cahuilla Indians lived in this treeless desert area and adapted to the scarce environment. Instead of living on acorns and fish, which weren't plentiful, the Cahuilla lived on seeds, plants, and game. Cahuilla women made tea from mesquite pods and sometimes stored it in an *olla*. *

prehistoric olla

Cahuilla woman

wind turbine

roadrunner

round-tailed squirrel

Many historians think the name California comes from a romantic Spanish fiction story called "Las Sergas de Esplandián" ("The Exploits of Esplandián") by Garcí Ordóñez de Montalvo, published in 1510. The story is about an imaginary, treasure-filled island called California that was not far from "Terrestrial Paradise" and was ruled by Queen Calafia. When Spanish explorers discovered the Pacific Coast north of Mexico, sometime in the 1530s or 1540s, they called it California after the island in the story.

California state flag

California state seal

*California state insect—
dogface butterfly*

*California state flower—
golden poppy*

*California state tree—
great redwood*

*California state mineral—
gold*

*California state marine mammal—
gray whale*

*California state animal—
grizzly bear*

*California state bird—
quail*